RADICAL JESUS

Dennis Meaker

CONTENTS

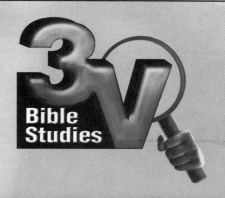

About

This Bible study focuses on three key tools for exciting Bible study: comprehension, interpretation, and application.

WHAT'S THE TEXT? begins by simply reading the Scripture passage for what it says. Then it invites deeper understanding by having us examine and ask questions about the text.

WHAT'S THE CONTEXT? looks at both the literary issues and the cultural and social situation. The information in this section may address specific terms used in the passage, the character of the particular book of the Bible, what comes before the passage, what comes after it, and the events and cultural expectations of the times. Having this "story behind the story" provides important information for understanding the text and its meaning.

WHAT'S NEXT?, the third section, recognizes that studying the Bible is not focused on information, but on transformation. Here's where we intentionally focus on today by looking at different "Views" that relate to contemporary life.

One reason for doing Bible study this way is to learn *how* to study the Bible. As your group works through text, context, and what's next, you will be learning an important skill for a lifetime of encountering God's Word.

The real joy in engaging this Living Word is its power to change our lives—for the better. You don't have to get "right" answers; you do have to be open and searching—and the Spirit will lead you.

Visit www.ileadyouth.com/3V for
- student-leader helps
- background on the Gospels
- worship suggestions
- contents of the other studies in the 3V series

Leading the Studies

Adult and Student Leaders

Adults or high school students can lead or co-lead these studies. Interested students can facilitate the whole study or lead a particular discussion or activity for their peers. By using small groups at particular points, all students will gain more experience as both leaders and participants.

Students who have been student-leaders for *Synago* are especially qualified to lead all or portions of these 3V Bible Studies. Go to *www.ileadyouth.com* for student-leader helps and for more information about *Synago* for senior highs.

Activities

As you lead, don't hesitate to try some of the more active ideas (roleplay or drawing, for example). Sometimes the physical and verbal cues of a one-minute roleplay lead to great new insights. Another reason to try the activities is that different people learn in different ways. So expand the opportunities for everyone to learn.

Group Size

All size groups of senior highs can easily use this study method. If your group is small, do most of the sections together, with occasional conversations in pairs or threes. If the group is larger, break into small groups or pairs more often, with times of reporting and talking as a whole group.

Bibles

Everyone should have access to a study book and a Bible. Have a variety of translations of the Bible available. Referring to the different translations is a helpful skill in Bible study. Sometimes subtle nuances in the wording can give more clarity or insight. Sometimes they help raise good questions.

The New Revised Standard Version (NRSV) is printed here so that students can feel good about writing in their books. They can highlight words and phrases they think are important or note questions that the Scripture passage raises for them, which they might not do in a Bible.

FITTING YOUR TIME

This approach to Bible study is very flexible. You may choose to:

- **Do all of a particular study or streamline it;**
- **Do the study in one session or over two or three;**
- **Do all the questions, or choose some;**
- **Do some of the studies or all of them.**

If you need to spend less time, plan to do What's the Text? and What's the Context? You may wish to deal with fewer of the questions in each section. Be sure to do "After Looking at Both the Text and the Context...."

If you have more time, add "View You" in What's Next? If you have still more time, use one or all of the other Views (A, B, C) for some spirited debate.

Suggested Schedule Options

One Session Only

5–10 minutes	What's the Text?
20–25	What's the Context? (Selected Questions)
20–35	What's Next? (Selected Views)
5–10	View You

Two Sessions

10–15 minutes	What's the Text?
20–30	What's the Context? (Selected Questions)
10–15	What's Next (One View)
10–15 minutes	Review of Text and Context
30–40	What's Next? (Remaining Views)
5–10	View You

Three Sessions

1. Do What's the Text? and What's the Context? (Most Questions)
2. Do a review of Text and Context; finish any remaining Context sections and After Looking at Both the Text and the Context.
3. Do a brief review of previous sessions; choose one or more of the Views in What's Next? Close with View You.

TESTING JESUS
MATTHEW 4:1-11

Have you ever been referred to as the son or daughter of one of your parents? For instance, someone might say, "That's Frank's son" or "That's Beth's daughter." While it can be wrong and unfair, some people will judge you and have expectations about you, based upon who your parents are. Imagine what it must have been like for Jesus, the Son of God. The story of the temptation or testing of Jesus explores the question, What kind of Son will Jesus be?

1

2

¹ Then Jesus was led up by the Spirit into the wilderness to be tempted by the devil. ² He fasted forty days and forty nights, and afterwards he was famished. 3 The tempter came and said to him, "If you are the Son of God, command these stones to become loaves of bread."

4 But he answered, "It is written,

'One does not live by bread alone,
 but by every word that comes from the mouth of God.'"

5 Then the devil took him to the holy city and placed him on the pinnacle of the temple, ⁶ saying to him, "If you are the Son of God, throw yourself down; for it is written,

'He will command his angels concerning you,'
 and 'On their hands they will bear you up,
so that you will not dash your foot against a stone.'"

7 Jesus said to him, "Again, it is written,

'Do not put the Lord your God to the test.'"

⁸ Again, the devil took him to a very high mountain and showed him all the kingdoms of the world and their splendor; 9 and he said to him, "All these I will give you, if you will fall down and worship me." ¹⁰ Jesus said to him, "Away with you, Satan! for it is written,

'Worship the Lord your God, and serve only him.'"

¹¹ Then the devil left him, and suddenly angels came and waited on him.

Matthew 4:1-11, NRSV
(Also Mark 1:12-13; Luke 4:1-13)

Read the passage aloud. Have others read silently from different translations of the Bible. Quickly, read the accounts in the other Gospels (Mark and Luke). Report any differences in the wording or events.

- How do the differences help you understand the text?
- What questions do the differences raise for you?

Have everyone highlight words or phrases in the text that they feel are important or that raise questions for them. For now, just list the highlighted words and phrases and the questions.

Invite volunteers to present the three tests visually to the group, acting out, pantomiming, or drawing the encounter. Use verses 3-4, 5-7, and 8-10.

- What stood out in seeing the story that you didn't think about earlier?
- What new questions does this experience with the text raise for you?

Add the new highlights and questions to the list.

RADICAL JESUS

4

WHAT'S THE CONTEXT?

As a whole group, read through this information and discuss the questions; **OR** read and discuss the commentaries in small groups or pairs assigned to a specific section or sections. Then summarize your conversation for the others.

The Gospel of Matthew

The Jesus you encounter in Matthew is a faithful Jew. Matthew was writing primarily to a Jewish audience. Connecting Jesus to their tradition and hopes for a messiah was important for convincing them of who Jesus was. For Matthew, Jesus was the fulfillment of Torah (the Law) and the prophets (Matthew 5:17). In fact, Matthew tells us repeatedly that things happened during Jesus' life and ministry to fulfill Scripture. (Look up Matthew 1:22, 2:15, 3:17.)

Look also at Matthew's genealogy of Jesus (Matthew 1:1-17).

- To whom does Matthew trace Jesus' ancestry?
- Why would that be significant to the Jews, who were Matthew's primary audience?

Matthew also emphasizes similarities between Jesus and Moses, the lawgiver of Israel. Jesus and Moses were born in humble surroundings, but both became great leaders. Jesus and Moses were both threatened with murder as babies. Moses fled from Egypt; Jesus and his family fled to Egypt. Moses gave the people the Law, received from God, on Mt. Horeb. Jesus gave the Sermon on the Mount, interpreting the law, and was the fulfillment of the Law.

Before and After

Scan Chapter 3 and the rest of Chapter 4 in Matthew.

- What happens before and after the testing of Jesus?
- Why do you think it might be significant for the story to be placed here? What relationships in the events do you see?

If you have more time, compare the placement of this story in Mark 1:12-13 and Luke 4:1-13 also.

Torah

Christians often misunderstand the purpose of the Law, or Torah, in the life of Israel. Torah is sometimes portrayed in the New Testament as a burden. However, Jews, in general, did not, and do not today, perceive Torah as such. Following Torah is an obligation owed to God and a privilege for Jews. Following Torah, being a holy people, would make the people of Israel a light for the nations (Matthew 5:14).

Read the following passages of Scripture: Psalm 1:1-3; Psalm 15:7-10; Psalm 119:72, 174.

- How is the Law described? To what is it compared?

In Matthew 5:17, Jesus says that he has come not to change the Law, but to fulfill it.

- What do you think he means?

Paul reminds us that, even though Christians are under grace, and not law, we are not free to do what we will. Read Romans 6:15-23; 1 Corinthians 9:21.

- What are your views on following the law of God? Is it a burden? or a help? something in between? Why?

RADICAL JESUS

The Call to Be a Just and Holy People

Christians may think of the dietary laws, laws relating to sacrifice, or laws relating to purity when they think of Torah. Those laws are prominent in the books of Deuteronomy and Leviticus, and they seem quite strange to us today.

Laws relating to these matters served several purposes, the most important of which were to set the people of Israel apart from the other people of the area and to keep reminding them of their covenant relationship with God. But Torah is much more than laws relating to diet or ritual cleansing. Torah called the people of Israel to be a holy people—a people who would be a blessing to all nations. (See Genesis 18:18; Deuteronomy 28:9; Isaiah 42:6.)

The people of Israel were to act with justice toward all people, even the aliens or foreigners who lived among them (Leviticus 19:33). Torah reminded Israel that, just as God heard their cries when they were oppressed in Egypt, so God would hear the cries of those whom Israel oppressed (Exodus 22:21-23).

When the prophets spoke about the heart of the Law, they did not focus upon diet and ritual; they spoke of justice and compassion. Amos admonishes the people to "hate evil and love good" (Amos 5:15). Justice and righteousness should flow from the people like rivers and streams (Amos 5:24). The Lord does not require ritual sacrifice, but the sacrifice of our pride and the acknowledgment of our sin (Psalm 51:17).

As you study the words of Jesus, especially those critical of Torah, understand that Jesus is an "insider," a Jew, speaking, in the tradition of the prophets, against an interpretation of the law that does not focus on justice and righteous living.

- What were two key reasons for the Law?
- What does it mean to you to live a holy life?
- Does it make you uncomfortable to think of yourself as holy? Why?

The Testing/Temptation of Jesus

This text is often called the Temptation of Jesus, but it is more appropriate to think of it as the Testing of Jesus. Moreover, unlike the portrayal of the temptation of Eve in Genesis, notice that the Spirit leads Jesus into the wilderness to encounter Satan. Satan does not seek Jesus out behind God's back. Matthew affirms that Satan is not a separate, co-equal, evil god. Satan is, ultimately, under the authority of God and can be used by God for God's own purposes.

Historically, the wilderness is a place of testing covenant faithfulness. The people wandered in the wilderness before being brought to the promised land, and Jesus is sent to the wilderness to be tested. The area is a desolate tract—a place of sandy hills, small mountains and rocks. Think of a place that looks much like any desert of the southwestern United States.

The repeated refrain, "If you are the Son of God . . ." should not be read to mean that Satan was challenging that Jesus was the Son of God. Matthew has already made it clear that Jesus is the Son of God, even noting that God claimed him as such at his baptism. However, just as people might want to know whether you are like your parents, so Satan is seeking to know just what kind of Son Jesus will be.

Was the test rigged? Some will insist that Jesus, being both human and divine, had a special advantage—a special power to resist temptation that ordinary humans could never have. This view is contrary to Christian teaching. Have someone read aloud Hebrews 4:14-16.

- What does the Hebrews passage say that relates to the text being studied?
- How does knowing the story of the temptation help you trust Jesus with your own issues?

WHAT MAKES SOMETHING A TEMPTATION?

- What comes to mind when you think of a temptation?
- Is it all bad? all good?

Often things that tempt us are appealing because they offer something good, something that fits our desires and our values. But upon closer look, the temptation may have costs or consequences that are not so good.

- What are things you hope for?
- What are things you desire?
- What would you do to get those things?
- What would you give up to get the things you hope for or desire?
- What "price" would you be willing to pay? What "price" would be too much?

FIRST TEST

- What was the nature of the test?
- What was really at stake?
- Why might this test be the very first test?
- Look up Deuteronomy 8:1-10. How does this text help you understand both the test and Jesus' answer to Satan?

Second Test

- What was the nature of the test?
- What was really at stake?
- What does it mean to test God? Do you think that testing God is a bad thing or unreasonable?
- Compare Deuteronomy 6:16 and Exodus 17:1-20 with Judges 6:36-40 and 1 Kings 18:20-39. How are the "tests of God" engaged in by Gideon and Elijah different from the one described in Deuteronomy, Exodus, and Matthew? In what ways are they the same?
- How would people today be affected if they saw a seemingly supernatural sign from God, such as someone jumping down from a high place and not being hurt or being saved by angels?
- Do you think that signs from God would bring more people into the church? Would more people believe in God if they could see some signs?
- How would signs from God affect your faith?
- Are miraculous signs necessary for people to have faith?

Third Test

In the last test, Jesus is offered a kingdom here on earth. Think of Jesus as being offered the presidency, the premiership, the role of absolute ruler of all nations on earth. The world would have no need for a United Nations, no wars, no inequities—one world government under the leadership of Jesus Christ.

- What is wrong with that?
- What would this offer cost Jesus?
- Why would the price be too much if he could do so much good?

After Looking at Both the Text and the Context . . .

> Deal with some or all of these questions before
> moving to What's Next?

- What new insights do you have?

- What stands out to you in the story now?

- What answers have you gained to the questions you raised earlier?

- What new questions do you have?

- In what ways do you identify with Jesus? with the tempter?

- Which of the tests do you personally struggle with most?

- In what other ways are you being tempted?

- If you had to describe to someone the kind of Son Jesus was, what would you say?

- What one learning do you take from this Scripture that you will remember and apply to your life?

Choose one or more of Views A, B, and C to discuss; **OR** have different small groups talk about one and then summarize the discussion for the other groups. **Be sure to have everyone complete View You.**

VIEW A
If Only I Were in Charge

Individually or in small groups, create a master plan for running the world. Base the plan on whatever criteria you choose.

- What would your world be like?
- What problems did you encounter as you planned a perfect world?

An appealing temptation is to take charge and fix things. If only we were in charge, things would be different. That is the third test Jesus endured—the test to put himself in charge of directing things here on earth. We might like such power. Yet how would we deal with the free will that God has granted every person?

Assume that your group has taken Satan up on his offer to preside over the nations of the world (but still refusing to worship Satan):

- How would you change the way things are run?
- How would you enforce your authority?
- How would you make your governance one that emphasized the work of God in the world?
- How would you deal with those who do not believe in God or who believe different things about God?

12

If Only I Could Change Things

Take a closer look at the first test: the temptation of Jesus to misuse the power he controlled. As portrayed, Jesus was invited to misuse his power for his own benefit, but would the outcome have been any different if he had been invited to use his power to feed the masses?

Although the Scriptures describe several feeding miracles, they do not show Jesus ending all hunger with a wave of his hand. Jesus opted to focus on those things that he discerned God was calling him to do. Even if we had the power to change things to suit us, things might not work out as we would have them. Try this:

- List those things that you think you would like to change with a wave of the hand, calling on the power of God to make changes like turning stones to bread. The only limitation on your power is that you may act on only those things you can see. You cannot, with a wave of the hand, eradicate world hunger; but you could create food for those you see. You cannot, with a wave of the hand, stop all wars; but you can affect violence that takes place in your presence.

- After people have had a chance to think about what they would do, talk as a group about the effects, positive and negative, of using God's power in that way.
- How would having such power affect your beliefs about God?

Who Is This Guy Satan?

There are two views about Satan prominent in the church today. One holds that Satan is an entity as real as God. The other holds that Satan is not to be understood as a being, but as a symbol of the forces of chaos and evil in the world.

• Take some time to discuss the views of those in the group about what they understand to be the nature of Satan: actual entity or merely the personification of evil and chaos.

However Satan is understood, this text has a powerful statement to make about Satan/evil. Satan, and what we perceive as evil, is, ultimately, under the authority of God. In this text, for instance, Satan is an instrument of God's will, used to test Jesus.

• If God has authority over Satan or the evil forces in the world, why is evil allowed to exist?
• How does God use or turn evil for God's purposes?
• Can good exist without evil?

RADICAL JESUS

 *View You*

Reread this Scripture (Matthew 4:1-11), and then pray the Lord's Prayer.

- Did you hear with new understanding the petition of the Lord's Prayer, "Lead me not into temptation" (or in some translations, such as the NRSV, "Lead me not to the time of trial")?

God may not be putting temptations in your path, but our faith is often tested each and every day by the complexities of living. Think back over your life and write a few words here that remind you of times your faith has been tested and you "passed" and times you have "failed."

In this space, or on a sheet of paper, write your reflections about this question: How is God speaking to me today through this Word?

"YOU HAVE HEARD IT SAID . . . BUT I SAY . . ."
MATTHEW 5:38-48

"Love your enemies." "Turn the other cheek." "Do not resist an evil doer." Talk about hard commandments! Yet the plain meaning of these Scriptures couldn't be clearer. Or could it?

38 "You have heard that it was said, 'An eye for an eye and a tooth for a tooth.' 39 But I say to you, Do not resist an evildoer. But if anyone strikes you on the right cheek, turn the other also; 40 and if anyone wants to sue you and take your coat, give your cloak as well; 41 and if anyone forces you to go one mile, go also the second mile. 42 Give to everyone who begs from you, and do not refuse anyone who wants to borrow from you.

43 "You have heard that it was said, 'You shall love your neighbor and hate your enemy.' 44 But I say to you, Love your enemies and pray for those who persecute you, 45 so that you may be children of your Father in heaven; for [God] makes his sun rise on the evil and on the good, and sends rain on the righteous and on the unrighteous. 46 For if you love those who love you, what reward do you have? 47 And if you greet only your brothers and sisters, what more are you doing than others? 48 Be perfect, therefore, as your heavenly Father is perfect."

Matthew 5:38-48, NRSV
(Also Luke 6:27-36)

Read the passage aloud. Have others read silently from different translations of the Bible. Report any differences.

• How do the differences help you understand the text?

Make a list of the all the unexpected and radical things that Jesus says we are to do.

• What questions does the text raise for you? List those.

As a whole group, read through this information and discuss the questions; **OR** read and discuss the commentaries in small groups or pairs assigned to a specific section or sections. Then summarize your conversation for the others.

SERMON ON THE MOUNT

Look at Matthew 5:1, and scan the teachings of Jesus given in chapters 5-7. Today's passage is part of the larger text referred to as the Sermon on the Mount. Likely, Jesus said very similar things everywhere he went. (You may wish to compare today's passage with the Sermon on the Plain in Luke 6:27-36.)

• Why would Matthew describe a mountainside setting where Jesus spoke about the Law? Who else spoke of the Law in a mountain setting?
• Why would it be important for Matthew to make that connection for his audience?

Placed near the beginning of the Gospel, the Sermon on the Mount also provides a benchmark. From this point forward, the reader is invited to judge the actions of Jesus and his disciples against his teachings.

• From your knowledge of Jesus, how well did he measure up to his own teachings? Give specific examples.

RADICAL JESUS

The Plain Meaning

The Scriptures were written in Hebrew, Greek, and Aramaic in a specific time and place. In order to understand the Scripture and hear God's Word for our lives today, we need to consider the meanings the words had and try to understand the societal context that existed when they were spoken and written.

Split into pairs (or threes). One person should assume the role of a person who speaks and reads only a little English. The other person's (persons') task is to explain the following paragraph. Watch out for words in which the meaning shifts (*lead, deck, foot*), words that look similar but that have different meanings (*lead, leader and leadership; weigh, weight, and weighed; pounds and pounding*), and usages that require an understanding of our culture and society in the United States (*fire department, EPA*).

The massive lead weight covered a square foot of the deck and had to be moved. Sam asked how much the weight weighed, but no one knew. Sam guessed 200 pounds. Cindy kicked at the weight a while with her foot, lost in thought. Sarah, the leader of the group, was weighed down by the responsibility of leadership. She stood a foot away from the weight, absently pounding on her leg. Everyone looked to her to lead the way. She thought that disposing of the lead weight might require the help of the fire department or advice from the EPA. Gregg, unconcerned as ever, was playing with a deck of cards at the foot of the stairs.

As this exercise illustrates, "the plain meaning" is slippery if you are not familiar with the language and the culture that created the statement. Those problems can be even greater when the culture is gone and the language has not been in common use for thousands of years. This passage from Matthew, in particular, uses references that would have been familiar to the crowds who heard Jesus but are less familiar to us.

"An Eye for an Eye"

- What do people usually mean when they use the phrase "an eye for an eye..."?

The rule of "an eye for an eye, a tooth for a tooth," is found in Exodus 21:24 (also in Leviticus 24:20 and Deuteronomy 19:21). As harsh as it sounds to our ears, it was actually meant for good. The rule restrained people's responses. If someone killed your brother, then your family might kill the killer but not his or her whole family. "An eye for an eye" was meant to stop unlimited retribution.

- How does this information change for you the usual understanding of the phrase "an eye for an eye"?
- What do you think Jesus is saying about retaliation?

"If Anyone Strikes You . . ."

Have you ever seen an old movie where one person takes a glove and slaps another in the face? or watched the drama of "the slap" on a soap opera? Striking someone on the cheek was a form of insult, showing your contempt for that person. For centuries, such insults resulted in duels or fights. Jesus is describing not a fight, but one person publicly humiliating another, possibly with a slap from the back of the hand. His instruction to turn the other cheek is, in effect, to accept the humiliation without responding in kind.

- In what ways do people insult one another?
- Among your friends and acquaintances, how do people respond to being insulted or disrespected?
- What are the usual consequences of their responses?
- What would be the likely consequences of following Jesus' instruction?

"If Anyone Wants to Sue You . . ."

The "courts" of Jesus' day were not courts as we generally think of them. They were more like the *Judge Judy* television show. Court was held near the public gates and provided great shows. People would bring their witnesses and plead their cases. The justice dispensed was swift.

Jesus describes a fictional lawsuit where someone sues for a person's coat, and Jesus instructs the defendant to give over the cloak as well. A cloak could not, by law, be taken; because it might be the only garment that would keep the person from freezing to death. Jesus advises not only not resisting the lawsuit, but giving up what the law could not take.

- Imagine that your family is being sued. What factors would make you want to resist the lawsuit? Would the level of your resistance depend upon the amount of money involved?
- Would you want to follow Jesus' advice and not resist the lawsuit. Why, or why not?
- If you did not resist, what might the effect be on the complainant?

"If Anyone Forces You to Walk a Mile . . ."

Judea and Galilee were occupied by Rome. A Roman soldier could force someone to carry his burdens a prescribed distance. Like being slapped in the face, such a task was humiliating for the person forced to work for the Roman soldier and the hated empire he represented.

- Roleplay the situation. How would the choice to go the second mile affect the one who forced the first mile of service?
- Quickly roleplay an alternative. What would happen if you refused to do what was required or turned on the oppressor after completing the first mile? How much likelihood would there be of changing the oppressor?
- Why do you think Jesus advised the people not only to not resist this demand, but to walk the extra mile?
- "Going the extra mile" is a phrase commonly used today. Is it used today the way Jesus uses it here?
- In what situations today would Jesus' counsel be an appropriate response?

"Give to Anyone Who Begs From You . . ."

The command to give to anyone who begs from you reflects a strong bias in Torah to share with those who are in need the blessings you have received. On the surface, it seems out of place with the other passages.

- What feelings do you experience in such situations?
- How is responding to someone begging from you like the other examples Jesus uses?

RADICAL JESUS

RADICAL JESUS

"HATE YOUR ENEMY"?

Eugene Peterson's *The Message* translates verse 43 this way: "You're familiar with the old written law, 'Love your friend' and its unwritten companion, 'Hate your enemy.'" Jesus is probably referring to just such an unwritten law. (Nowhere in the Old Testament are the people instructed to hate their enemies.) However, people *want* to hate their enemies. Instead, Jesus calls upon us to love our enemies. After all, it's easy to love someone you like. Everyone can do that.

- Does loving your enemies mean that you feel affection for those who hurt you?
- What does this statement mean to you in light of this passage: "Love is a decision"?
- Loving our enemies can be a means of helping them understand what it means to be a Christian. It might even lead the persons to follow Jesus. But what if no such life change occurs? Are we to continue loving such an "enemy"?
- Whom do you consider to be your enemies? How do you interpret this command to love them?
- What does Jesus mean when he calls upon us to be perfect the way God is perfect? Can we ever hope to be perfect like God?

After Looking at Both the Text and the Context . . .

> Deal with some or all of these questions before moving to What's Next?

- What new insights do you have?

- What stands out to you in these teachings now?

- What answers have you gained to the questions you raised earlier?

- What new questions do you have?

- How radical are these teachings? Why?

- Which of these teachings is easiest for you to follow? Which is hardest?

- If more Christians were to follow these teachings, how would life be different?

- What one learning do you take from this Scripture that you will remember and apply to your life?

Choose one or more of Views A, B, and C to discuss; **OR** have different small groups talk about one and then summarize the discussion for the other groups. **Be sure to have everyone complete View You.**

VIEW A — Breaking the Violence Cycle

"Don't get mad—get even!" That popular bumper sticker also expresses a view held by some people. As a joke, it's amusing. In real life, it can quickly become ugly. Someone is hurt and strikes back. The person struck, or someone close to him or her, retaliates. And so on. Thus the cycle of violence escalates.

Life is full of opportunities to hurt someone intentionally or unintentionally. Depending upon the response of the person hurt, the situation can quickly get out of hand. Christians are called to reject a life philosophy that perpetuates the harm and, instead, act to stop the hurt.

Working in small groups, make a list of examples people have experienced, witnessed, or heard about where someone was publicly humiliated or attacked by another. Do not limit yourself to situations in school or among your peers. Consider the conduct of prominent adults, including politicians, sports figures, or other people in the news. Use examples from movies or books too.

- How did that person act?
- What were the consequences?
- What could have been done to make the situation better?

Roleplay a situation in which a peer is insulting you.

- How can you respond to the situation in a way that doesn't make it worse?
- What happens if the person simply won't stop the bad behavior?

"Give to everyone who begs from you, and do not refuse anyone who wants to borrow from you." There is a strong theme in the Old and New Testaments encouraging people to give generously to those who are less fortunate. Yet what about our own needs?

- Have you ever walked the streets of a city where people approached and asked for money? How did that make you feel? Were you angry or afraid? Did you feel uncomfortable being asked for money?
- Did you refuse to give any money, even though you had money to give? Why?
- If you gave away money, why did you? How did that make you feel?
- Under what circumstances would you and the members of the group be willing to give freely of what you own, even if it meant that you would have to do without something that you really wanted? or something you really needed?
- What do you think are some of the needs that have resulted in the action of begging?
- How might those needs be addressed? What might these people require other than a handout?
- What could you give instead of money?

RADICAL JESUS

Love Those Trying to Kill Us?

"Do not resist evil doers." "Love your enemies." Those commandments have taken on new meaning in the United States and the world since September 11, 2001. How do we follow these commandments when confronting people who apparently believe just as strongly that God wishes for them to kill us?

The examples used by Jesus in this text do not include examples of people standing by and doing nothing while another is harmed. They all deal with the individual response to a humiliating situation. Based on that omission, some commentators do not think that Jesus would have expected us to act non-violently in the face of evil like the September 11 bombings.

On the other hand, many Christians over the centuries have interpreted the words of Jesus in these verses as a command to refuse to resort to force, even in the face of evil. Looking to the plain meaning of the text, acknowledging the ambiguities involved in determining plain meaning, they believe that violence can never serve the will of God. Such people do oppose evil, and often at the cost of their lives. But they will not resort to violence.

One example of non-violent resistance to evil is the resistance of the people of India, under the leadership of Mahatma Gandhi, against British Rule of their country prior to and following the Second World War. Another is the resistance of African-Americans during the 1950s and '60s against the laws mandating segregation.

- Given what you know of these events, how do you think you would have responded to these situations if you had lived in those times and places? Would you have chosen non-violence, or engaged in violent action to protest the evil you saw?

The United States, in response to September 11, has chosen to pursue the so-called War on Terror and the war on Iraq (Operation Iraqi Freedom). Working in small groups, and then as a whole, list the benefits and costs of one or both of these wars as you perceive them.

- What has been accomplished?
- What has been the cost in lives harmed, lives lost, and property destroyed? Consider all of the effects of war: the disease and starvation that often follows in the wake of war, the lost opportunities, the destroyed families. List these for *both* sides involved.

As the church, the body of Christ, we are called to try to discern the will of God in all matters and try to act in accordance with God's will. Yet as a sinful people, we often have a difficult time discerning what the will of God is in a particular situation.

- Based upon your perceptions, in what ways has the War on Terror or the war on Iraq served the will of God?
- In what ways has it been a disservice?
- What alternatives to war are there that provide a stand against evil without creating more evil and destruction?

If your church has a statement about the use of military power and war, distribute copies and discuss that statement.

- Has the statement ever been a topic of a sermon in your church?
- Do you think that your church's position on these issues are in agreement with the views of people in your congregation?
- At what points do you agree (or disagree or find yourself struggling) with your church's statement?

Like many of Jesus' teachings, this one is not easy. It's OK to struggle with its meaning for you, but continue to stay open to the Spirit's guidance and pray for clarity around these teachings.

- What new questions does this reading and discussion raise for you?
- What commitments are you willing to make or reaffirm based on this reading and discussion?

RADICAL JESUS

View You

Picture in your mind a person who has hurt you. For three or four minutes, simply hold that person's image in your mind, trying to see him or her as someone other than an enemy. Then pray that God might help you come to understand this person and to care about his or her well-being. You can pray as well for any change in the behavior of the person that you would like to see, but make the primary focus of your prayer that God would help *you* better understand that person—that God would help you to love this person, not necessarily with affection, but with a concern for her or his well-being.

In this space, or on a sheet of paper, write your reflections about this question: How is God speaking to me today through this Word?

Healing the Paralyzed Man
Mark 2:1-12

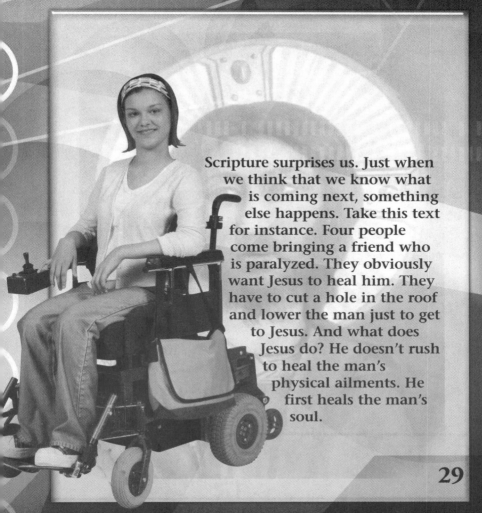

Scripture surprises us. Just when we think that we know what is coming next, something else happens. Take this text for instance. Four people come bringing a friend who is paralyzed. They obviously want Jesus to heal him. They have to cut a hole in the roof and lower the man just to get to Jesus. And what does Jesus do? He doesn't rush to heal the man's physical ailments. He first heals the man's soul.

1 When he returned to Capernaum after some days, it was reported that he was at home. 2 So many gathered around that there was no longer room for them, not even in front of the door; and he was speaking the word to them. 3 Then some people came, bringing to him a paralyzed man, carried by four of them. 4 And when they could not bring him to Jesus because of the crowd, they removed the roof above him; and after having dug through it, they let down the mat on which the paralytic lay. 5 When Jesus saw their faith, he said to the paralytic, "Son, your sins are forgiven."

6 Now some of the scribes were sitting there, questioning in their hearts, 7 "Why does this fellow speak in this way? It is blasphemy! Who can forgive sins but God alone?"

8 At once Jesus perceived in his spirit that they were discussing these questions among themselves; and he said to them, "Why do you raise such questions in your hearts? 9 Which is easier, to say to the paralytic, 'Your sins are forgiven,' or to say, 'Stand up and take your mat and walk'? 10 But so that you may know that the Son of Man has authority on earth to forgive sins"—he said to the paralytic—11 "I say to you, stand up, take your mat and go to your home." 12 And he stood up, and immediately took the mat and went out before all of them; so that they were all amazed and glorified God, saying, "We have never seen anything like this!"

Mark 2:1-12, NRSV
(Also Matthew 9:2-8
and Luke 5:17-26)

Read the passage aloud. Have two other volunteers read the different versions in Matthew 9:2-8 and Luke 5:17-26.

- What are the differences?
- How do the differences help you understand the text?
- What questions do the differences raise for you?

Have everyone highlight words or phrases in the text that they feel are important or that raise questions for them. List the highlighted words and phrases and the questions. You may want to define words, if needed, but leave the questions and the significance of the highlighted items to be addressed over the course of the study.

Invite volunteers to present the story visually to the group, acting out, pantomiming, or drawing the various scenes. You may want to do verses 1-5 and 6-12 as two mini-dramas with two different sets of volunteers.

- What stood out in seeing the story that you didn't think about earlier?
- What new questions does this experience with the text raise for you?

Add the new highlights and questions to the list.

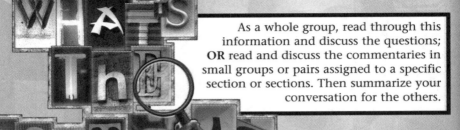

As a whole group, read through this information and discuss the questions; **OR** read and discuss the commentaries in small groups or pairs assigned to a specific section or sections. Then summarize your conversation for the others.

MARK'S EMPHASES

The Gospel of Mark could be subtitled "Sprinting Through Judea and Galilee With Jesus." When you read the Gospel of Mark, get ready to move fast. Mark jumps from place to place, always moving "immediately."

• For fun, scan the Gospel or a concordance to see how many times the word *immediately* appears in this short book.

A lot takes place in a short time. Here it is, only Chapter 2, and Jesus has already been baptized, been tested, started his ministry of preaching, started calling his disciples, cast out a demon in Capernaum, cured Simon's mother-in-law and many others who were brought to the house, took a preaching tour of towns in the Galilee, cast out some more demons, and cured a man of leprosy. Whew!

• Look at Mark 1:14-15. What is Jesus' key message?
• What does the word *repent* mean? How does that relate to God?
• Why would that be an important emphasis of this Gospel?

The Problem of Sin

When people think of sin, they most often think of things that they do that harm themselves or others. People sometimes say of sin, "I know it when I see it."

- Make a list of those activities that people think of as sins and anything else that people believe is a sin. Don't be surprised if there is disagreement on some sins. Flag the sins for further discussion. If possible, write the list where people can see it and refer to it later.

Making lists of sins can become quite cumbersome—and the lists may not get to the heart of the problem of sin. Think of sin as being separated from God, as losing our focus on and trust in God. This definition should cover all the actions on your list that involve hurting ourselves and others.

- Try this: Everyone stands in a circle. Imagine that at the center of the circle is God. Everyone takes a step closer to God. What happens to your relationships with the others in the circle? Now have everyone take two steps away from God. What happens to your relationships with people?
- Why would being separated from God (sin) affect how we treat other people? ourselves? creation?
- How do those things listed as sins separate us from God?

Read 1 John 4:20.

- How hard is it to love the God you can't see if you can't love the people you can see?
- Who are your brothers and sisters whom you are supposed to love?

RADICAL JESUS

Sins and Sickness

Look at the sin list developed in "The Problem of Sin" (page 33).

- Which of those sins could affect the health of the "sinner"? How?
- Is there a relationship between sin and health? Yes? No? Sometimes? Choose one answer and explain it.

Was the man's paralysis related to his sin? Possibly. We are not told. However, there is no reason to assume that was the case. Before and after this text, Jesus is described as healing people brought to him, without reference to his having to forgive their sins as well. We should take this story at face value. Jesus looked at the man and determined that his greatest problem was not his paralysis, but sin.

- What was the first healing in this story?
- What was the second?

Signs of God's Authority

Many of us are familiar with the stories of healing and other miracles in the New Testament. In the Gospels, such events are seen as signs that Jesus is the Messiah. However, the scribes in this story may be forgiven for not accepting healings as proof of Jesus as Messiah since some Old Testament prophets also healed, performed feeding miracles, and even raised people from the dead.

Read and compare the following Old Testament passages to the text from Mark. What were the miracles in these stories?

   1 Kings 17:8-24

   2 Kings 4:32-37

   2 Kings 4:42-44

   2 Kings 5:1-14

• If you were one of the scribes, what questions would you ask of Jesus to help you better understand how his authority from God is different from that of the prophets of old?

AFTER LOOKING AT BOTH THE TEXT AND THE CONTEXT . . .

> Deal with some or all of these questions before moving to What's Next?

- What new insights do you have?

- What stands out to you in the story now?

- What answers have you gained to the questions you raised earlier?

- What new questions do you have?

- In what ways do you identify with the paralyzed man? the scribes? the friends? the crowd?

- Have you or someone you know well experienced physical healing that was out of the ordinary? Tell about it.

- How have you experienced spiritual healing, forgiveness, being released from the power of sin?

- What one learning do you take from this Scripture that you will remember and apply to your life?

Choose one or more of Views A, B, and C to discuss; **OR** have different small groups talk about one and then summarize the discussion for the other groups. **Be sure to have everyone complete View You.**

VIEW A
THE HEALING of OUR SOULS

Jesus does not suggest that the man's paralysis is the result of the his sin; however, sin can cause sickness or disability.

• Refer to the sin list created earlier (page 33). Look it over and identify sins that might result in suffering illness and injury.

The Apostle Paul sometimes speaks in terms of sin as a power that can take control our lives. (For example, Romans 6:12.) The Old Testament also speaks of sin in much the same way. (See Genesis 4:7, where sin is described as like a creature lurking at your door.)

• In what ways do you see sin taking over lives of people you know or people in the news?
• How do you experience sin's presence? What image, like "lurking at your door" would you use to describe sin?

The concept of the forgiveness of sins includes a belief in the strengthening of a person's relationship with God. With the strengthening of that relationship comes the ability to resist the power that sin has over his or her life.

• How can the church be an instrument of God's healing as people struggle to overcome the power of sin in their lives?
• How can having Christian friends help you in dealing with the power of sin?

RADICAL JESUS

RADICAL JESUS

Faith Friends

A common statement in the New Testament is along the line of "Your faith has healed you." Note that in this Scripture passage, Jesus credits the faith of the four friends who brought the paralytic to him, not the faith of the man himself. Faithful people can have a powerful influence in our lives.

- Working first alone, then in small groups, and then as a whole group, identify people in your life and in the life of your church who have brought healing to you and others as a result of their faith.
- How have these persons shown themselves to be people of faith?

The four friends taking their friend to Jesus was a demonstration of their faith that Jesus could bring healing to the man.

- How do you show your friends that faith in Christ is part of your life?
- What friends would you like to "take to Jesus"?
- At this point in your life, do you need for your friends to "take you to Jesus" for physical or spiritual healing? Talk with your friends about your needs, and ask for their intercessory prayer on your behalf.

WHAT ABOUT PHYSICAL HEALING?

This story includes the healing of the paralyzed man; but based on the text, the man's physical healing might never have taken place if the scribes had not challenged Jesus about forgiving sins.

- What do you think the friends who brought the man to Jesus would have said and done if Jesus had not healed the man's paralysis?
- How would you have felt if you had placed such a friend before Jesus, only to have Jesus fail to provide the healing that *you* desired?
- List people you know in your group and your church who are in need of healing. Are there any persons who are chronically ill? Are there any persons with debilitating or terminal illnesses? How long have these people been ill?
- Why do you think God has not brought them physical healing?

We know that with life comes the certainty of death. Yet death is often a hard thing to accept, especially when the person who is dying of an illness or accident is young. By the example of Christ and the apostles, and the instruction of Scripture, we understand that we are to pray for physical healing as well as spiritual healing. But one of the great unanswered questions of faith is why that physical healing so often does not come.

- Why do you think there are not more "miraculous healings"?
- How do we live with unanswered prayer?
- Why do we pray if it doesn't always "work"?

View You

Spend some time in personal prayer for persons, including yourself, who are struggling with sin. Place them, and yourself, before Christ. Ask for forgiveness of your sins and for the healing in body and soul that you and your friends need.

One man of faith has said that prayer, even prayers for others, is something that we do to change us as much as to change others. We pray that God will bring us healing in our hearts and spirits as well as healing for our friends and those we care about, that God will help us deal with the pain of loss and help us minister to those in need. Refer again to the list you have made of people who are in need of healing. As a faith friend, carry each of these persons before Christ in prayer, asking for healing in body and healing in spirit.

In this space, or on a sheet of paper, write your reflections about this question: How is God speaking to me today through this Word?

The Rich Man and Lazarus

Luke 16:19-31

Do you have too much money? Is money getting in the way of your relationship with God and the world around you? The radical Jesus we encounter in the Gospel of Luke is constantly asking those questions.

[19] "There was a rich man who was dressed in purple and fine linen and who feasted sumptuously every day. [20] And at his gate lay a poor man named Lazarus, covered with sores, [21] who longed to satisfy his hunger with what fell from the rich man's table; even the dogs would come and lick his sores. [22] The poor man died and was carried away by the angels to be with Abraham. The rich man also died and was buried. [23] In Hades, where he was being tormented, he looked up and saw Abraham far away with Lazarus by his side.

[24] "He called out, 'Father Abraham, have mercy on me, and send Lazarus to dip the tip of his finger in water and cool my tongue; for I am in agony in these flames.'

[25] "But Abraham said, 'Child, remember that during your lifetime you received your good things, and Lazarus in like manner evil things; but now he is comforted here, and you are in agony. [26] Besides all this, between you and us a great chasm has been fixed, so that those who might want to pass from here to you cannot do so, and no one can cross from there to us.'

[27] "He said, 'Then father, I beg you to send him to my father's house—[28] for I have five brothers—that he may warn them, so that they will not also come into this place of torment.'

[29] "Abraham replied, 'They have Moses and the prophets; they should listen to them.'

[30] "He said, 'No, father Abraham; but if someone goes to them from the dead, they will repent.'

[31] "He said to him, 'If they do not listen to Moses and the prophets, neither will they be convinced even if someone rises from the dead.'"

Luke 16:19-31, NRSV

Read the passage aloud. Have others read silently from different translations of the Bible. Report any differences in the wording.

• How do the differences help you understand the text?
• What questions do the differences raise for you?

Have everyone highlight words or phrases in the text that they feel are important or that raise questions for them. For now, just list the highlighted words and phrases and the questions.

Invite volunteers to do a readers' theater of the story. (In this type of presentation the readers convey the emotion and nuances of the dialogue by their inflections and tone of voice as they read the printed text.) You will need a narrator, Father Abraham, and the Rich Man to read.

• What stood out in hearing the story that you didn't think about earlier?
• What new questions does this experience with the text raise for you?

Add the new highlights and questions to the list.

RADICAL JESUS

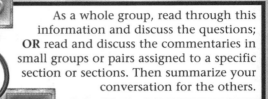

Luke's Emphases

Luke often touches on the themes of rich and poor. Look at what Mary says in the Magnificat (Luke 1:53); John the Baptist's statement about being saved (Luke 3:11); Jesus' definition of his ministry (Luke 4:18-19); Jesus' Sermon on the Plain (Luke 6:20-26), which is significantly different from the Sermon on the Mount (Matthew 5:3); Jesus' comment on another rich man and his treasure (Luke 12:13-21); and finally the choice Jesus lays out (Luke 16:13).

- Have different people read these passages silently and then summarize them for the group. What kinds of things does the Gospel writer emphasize about being rich and being poor? Do you agree or disagree with those concerns? Why, or why not?
- Do you think that you or your family are rich? If not, what would it take for you to feel rich?
- How can wealth become something we serve rather than God?
- How does it make you feel to hear the words of Jesus that those who are "rich" have received their consolation?

Later in the Gospel, following this parable, is the story of the rich ruler, who is unable to give up his possessions to follow Jesus (Luke 18:18-27). Jesus laments that it is difficult for the rich to enter the kingdom of God. "Then who can be saved," ask the disciples? And Jesus replies that with God, all things are possible.

As a whole group, read through this information and discuss the questions; **OR** read and discuss the commentaries in small groups or pairs assigned to a specific section or sections. Then summarize your conversation for the others.

Riches and Eyesight

The parable of Lazarus and the rich man is called a reversal story. By the end of the story, the characters have, in effect, traded places. The first part of the story sets the characters up for us. The rich man is a conspicuous consumer—think eight-car garage, with two cars for every space. He lives in a walled home, dresses in purple, and dines on the finest food. All of these facts would have told the first hearers of the story that this man was very wealthy indeed.

The walled home provided privacy and security, and the fact that the rich man dressed in purple indicates that he was part of a royal household or that he was a high government official. The Romans had laws dictating who could wear the color purple and how much they could wear, depending upon their station in life. The color purple was reserved for people of high rank.

Look again at the story.

- Does the rich man know that Lazarus is lying at his gate?
- Does the rich man really see Lazarus?
- How do people frequently react to a person who is obviously poor and perhaps diseased? Why?
- Even after death, how did the rich man relate to Lazarus? or did he relate to him?

Proverbs 18:11 states:

 The wealth of the rich is their strong city;
  in their imagination it is like a high wall.

- What do you think is the meaning of this proverb and its relationship to the parable of the rich man and Lazarus?
- What are ways people today erect a "high wall" between themselves and persons in need?

Abraham, Moses, and the Prophets

- Abraham is a key player in this story. Who is he? What do you recall about him? Read Genesis 12:1-4.

Abraham, through Isaac, Jacob, and Jacob's sons, is considered the patriarch, the ancestor, the father figure, for the people of Israel. He answered God's call and was the one with whom God initially entered into covenant. Paul describes him as a man of faith, righteous *without* the Law (Romans 4:1-12).

- What could the "brothers" learn from the example of Abraham?

Moses is a symbol for the Law—the Ten Commandments and the law built around those commandments. Many of those laws make provision for the poor. For example, the law called upon landowners to share their harvest with the poor (Leviticus 19:9-10).

- What lessons could the "brothers" learn by studying the Law?

The prophets of Israel called the people back to the intent of the Law and held them accountable for giving God true worship—practices that showed care for God's people, especially the poor and oppressed. Read Isaiah 58:6-7 and Micah 6:6-8.

- What could the "brothers" learn by listening to the prophets?

In this story, Abraham tells the rich man that even someone coming back from the dead won't be sufficient for the brothers if they cannot learn from Moses and the prophets.

- What do you think that statement means?
- Would the words of someone returning from the dead have an influence on you? Why, or why not?
- Whom do you know who did return from the dead? What influence does he have on the way you live and treat others?

Beliefs About the Afterlife

What is the nature of the afterlife? Where are we, and what do we experience after dying to this world? These questions have always captured the imagination of humans.

• Take some time to listen to one another's views on what you think you will experience after your life on earth is over.

Among Jews in the first century, there were at least two views of life after death. The first view, allegedly held by the Sadducees, was that there was no life after death. The soul perished along with the body. Those who die were no more. See, for example, Psalm 115:16-18. Compare it with Psalm 139:1-18.

Later traditions started to express a belief in a resurrection from the dead. Look at Isaiah 26:19 and Daniel 12:2. The Pharisees, another group of religious thinkers, believed in an eternal afterlife where God rewarded or punished.

Jesus clearly believed in the resurrection from the dead (Matthew 22:23-33). Several of Jesus' stories, like this one, refer to a time of punishment or reward following death. (See, for example, Matthew 25:46 and Luke 13:28.) Paul, in writing to the Corinthians, describes what he believes resurrection life will be like (1 Corinthians 15:35-38).

• After looking at these passages, again talk about your thoughts on life after death. Have any of your thoughts changed?
• How do your views about life after death influence how you live your life now? Or do they?

After Looking at Both the Text and the Context . . .

Deal with some or all of these questions before
moving to What's Next?

• What new insights do you have?

• What stands out to you in the story now?

• What answers have you gained to the questions you raised earlier?

• What new questions do you have?

• In what ways do you identify with Lazarus? the rich man?

• Whom do you think of as the "Lazaruses" in your life? as the "rich people"? Why?

• What one learning do you take from this Scripture that you will remember and apply to your life?

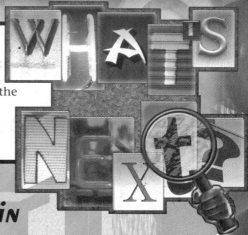

Choose one or more of Views A, B, and C to discuss; **OR** have different small groups talk about one and then summarize the discussion for the other groups. **Be sure to have everyone complete View You.**

VIEW A

Who's in Control?

A common view of this text is as a cautionary tale against letting your wealth become so much the focus of your life that you fail to listen for, and hear, the word of God. One way to keep a handle on this problem is to become aware of how much money you have.

- As a group, list things teenagers spend money on; for example, lunches, clothes, movies, CDs, cars. You don't have to tell anyone how much you have or spend, but be honest with yourself as you participate in this task.
- Once the list is complete, consider as a group what would be a reasonable amount to spend on these in a year.
- What was surprising to you about the figures? For instance, if you are buying your lunch from a fast-food vendor every day, you may be spending more than $100 a month on lunches—$1,200 a year. Is that too much? How about clothes? What is a reasonable amount to spend on clothes? Try to reach a consensus on how much is reasonable in your categories.
- Individually, compare the amount the group recommends with what you know you spend. What would you have to give up to take better control of your spending?
- Are you tithing—giving 1/10th of all you receive to your church for use in various ministries? Discuss as a group whether you would be willing to try tithing for three months. Are you willing, regardless of what the others decide?
- Ask your pastor what your church does to serve the poor and those in need in your local area. Discuss how you could help. How could your financial contribution help?

RADICAL JESUS

 **THE DESERVING POOR?**

A concept often thrown around is one of the "deserving poor." Many of us are willing to help people who are truly unable to help themselves, such as elderly widows and orphans; but we shy away from helping those whom we believe could take care of themselves or who have been, in some sense, the authors of their own misery.

Many welfare programs around the nation are being turned into "workfare" programs, where people are given assistance and job training help for a limited time and then left to fend for themselves. Whether or not the person has been adequately trained for employment, whether or not there are jobs available, they are cut off from assistance. Once they have received a prescribed level of help, they are no longer "deserving," in a legal sense, of additional help.

Yet this parable, and the Gospel of Luke, in general, has little interest in the reasons someone is in need of help.

- Examine this passage again. Why is Lazarus in this state? Is he responsible for his poverty and disease?
- What are our responsibilities to the poor? Should we make judgments about why people are in need of help, or simply help all without regard to their ability to help themselves?
- If you believe that we should distinguish between the deserving and undeserving poor, what criteria do you think are appropriate? What factors should be taken into account?
- Part of what we profess as Christians is that we have received the undeserved gift of the grace of God. Does that theological claim relate to this issue of how we are to respond to the poor? If so, in what ways?

Hospitality is another related and powerful theme in this Gospel. Luke tells a rich host that when he has a dinner, he should invite, not the rich, but the poor, the crippled, those who have been pushed to the edges of society—those who cannot repay him (Luke 14:12). In other words, don't simply give Lazarus the scraps off your table, but invite him into your home as an honored guest.

• Compare the conduct of the rich man with that of the Samaritan in Luke 10:25-37. How do you think the Samaritan would have dealt with Lazarus at his gate?

The United States, along with the other industrialized nations, such as Canada, England, countries in Western Europe, Australia, and Japan, at any given time consume the majority of the world's resources although they have less than one-quarter of the world's population. The remaining countries of the world, whose population is more than three times that of the developed nations, are left with too few resources. Even the poorest citizens of these richer countries are, by the standards of many of the poorer societies, quite wealthy. One way to visualize this discrepancy is to think of a pie. Twenty people get to eat 80% of the pie, and eighty people are left to share 20% of it.

In the United States, even before the attacks of September 11, 2001, immigration was controlled. Most of the wealthy nations limit immigration. Yet people illegally enter these countries every day, with the hope of a better life.

• Are we, like the rich man, turning a blind eye to Lazarus (the poorer nations of the world) at our gates?
• What would the radical Jesus we encounter in Luke tell us?
• What would we have to give up in order to welcome anyone who wanted to come to this country? or to increase the living standard of the poorer parts of our world?
• Is that something we should be praying to God to help make happen in our country?
• What has been your experience with immigrants? Why have they come here?
• How might you change the way you live to be more faithful?

View You

"I thought I was poor," is frequently a response from youth and adults returning from a mission trip. From their experiences of serving others in need, many Christians develop a clearer sense of how much they have and how little others make do with. They learn to see with new eyes their lives and the lives of others.

Take a few moments in meditation and prayer, thinking back over your activities last week. Where have you seen someone like Lazarus? How many people like Lazarus have you seen in the past week? Ask yourself what you need to do in your life to live for God and not for wealth.

In this space, or on a sheet of paper, write your reflections about this question: How is God speaking to me today through this Word?

A Loving Father With Two Difficult Children

Luke 15:11-32

Picture this conversation with your father and/or mother. You say, "Listen. I don't want to borrow the family car tonight. I want you to give me the car. And oh, by the way, since you'll probably give me a good part of your property after you die, I want that property now so that I can go out and make my way in the world. After all, it will be mine, won't it? I shouldn't have to wait for you to die, should I?" What do you suppose your parent(s) would say to you? That is the situation in the parable most often called the parable of the prodigal son.

11 Then Jesus said, "There was a man who had two sons. 12 The younger of them said to his father, 'Father, give me the share of the property that will belong to me.' So he divided his property between them. 13 A few days later the younger son gathered all he had and traveled to a distant country, and there he squandered his property in dissolute living. 14 When he had spent everything, a severe famine took place throughout that country, and he began to be in need. 15 So he went and hired himself out to one of the citizens of that country, who sent him to his fields to feed the pigs. 16 He would gladly have filled himself with the pods that the pigs were eating; and no one gave him anything. 17 But when he came to himself he said, 'How many of my father's hired hands have bread enough and to spare, but here I am dying of hunger! 18 I will get up and go to my father, and I will say to him, "Father, I have sinned against heaven and before you; 19 I am no longer worthy to be called your son; treat me like one of your hired hands."' 20 So he set off and went to his father. But while he was still far off, his father saw him and was filled with compassion; he ran and put his arms around him and kissed him.

21 Then the son said to him, 'Father, I have sinned against heaven and before you; I am no longer worthy to be called your son.' 22 But the father said to his slaves, 'Quickly, bring out a robe—the best one—and put it on him; put a ring on his finger and sandals on his feet. 23 And get the fatted calf and kill it, and let us eat and celebrate; 24 for this son of mine was dead and is alive again; he was lost and is found!' And they began to celebrate.

25 *"Now his elder son was in the field; and when he came and approached the house, he heard music and dancing.* 26 *He called one of the slaves and asked what was going on.* 27 *He replied, 'Your brother has come and your father has killed the fatted calf, because he has got him back safe and sound.'* 28 *Then he became angry and refused to go in. His father came out and began to plead with him.* 29 *But he answered his father, 'Listen! For all these years I have been working like a slave for you, and I have never disobeyed your command; yet you have never given me even a young goat so that I might celebrate with my friends.* 30 *But when this son of yours came back, who has devoured your property with prostitutes, you killed the fatted calf for him!'* 31 *Then the father said to him, 'Son, you are always with me, and all that is mine is yours.* 32 *But we had to celebrate and rejoice, because this brother of yours was dead and has come to life; he was lost and has been found.'"*

Luke 15:11-32, NRSV

Read the passage silently. Have everyone highlight words or phrases in the text that they feel are important or that raise questions for them. For now, just list the highlighted words and phrases and the questions.

Invite volunteers to give commentary on the likely thoughts and feelings of the characters, as someone reads the text again. You will need at least one person to speak the thoughts of the father, of the younger son, and of the older son. The reader should pause before the following verses for the volunteers to give their "inside commentary": 13, 14, 17, 20, 21, 22, 25, 28b, 29, 31. More than one person may add inside commentary for each character.

- What stood out in hearing the "inside commentary," the thoughts and feelings of the person, that you didn't think about earlier?
- What new questions does this experience with the text raise for you?

Add the new highlights and questions to the list.

RADICAL JESUS

WHAT'S THE CONTEXT?

As a whole group, read through this information and discuss the questions; **OR** read and discuss the commentaries in small groups or pairs assigned to a specific section or sections. Then summarize your conversation for the others.

COMPARING THE PARABLES

- What two parables come before this one? Describe them.
- How are they like this one?
- What do you think these three parables are about?
- Whom do the woman, the shepherd, and the father seem to represent?
- What do the coin, the 99 and 100th sheep, and the two brothers seem to represent?
- How is the role of the father different from that of the woman and the shepherd?
- What does that change seem to imply about the responsibility of the younger and older brothers, in contrast to the coin and the 100th sheep?

Distribute some hymnals and look at the hymn "Amazing Grace." Sing the hymn or read the words, paying careful attention to the active nature of God's grace that it proclaims.

- What experiences have you had of God reaching into your life?

Known as the parable of the prodigal son, this might better be called the parable of the loving father with *two* difficult sons. As you read and discuss the parable, try to look at the events from the viewpoint of all three main characters.

BROTHERS

Many Bible stories involve the interaction between brothers, with the younger brother often being the favored one of God. Read some of these stories, and talk about the relationship between the brothers:

Genesis 4:1-16 (Cain and Abel)
Genesis 25:19-34; 27; 32:3-21; 33:1-17 (Jacob and Esau)
Genesis 37:1-36 (Joseph and his brothers)

- Which brother do you like better? Why?
- What indications are there in these stories that God favored one brother over the other?
- Why might that be the case?

INHERITANCE

As the parable opens, the younger son asks his father for his "inheritance." The law in Deuteronomy 21:17 dictated that the elder son was entitled to a double portion from his father's estate. In this case, where there are two brothers and apparently no other heirs, the younger son would receive an inheritance of one third of the father's estate on his death.

The younger son is asking for what he will receive when his father dies. Such distributions were sometimes made when a younger son married so that he could support his new family. But early distributions were the exception, not the rule.

- Why do you think the younger son acted the way he did?
- Why would he ask for his inheritance from his father, in effect treating him as if he were dead?
- Why would he then leave the family?
- How would you feel if one of your brothers or sisters did something like that?

No One Gave Him Anything

Torah emphasized community—the responsibility that people had for one another's welfare. Torah reminded the people of Israel that once they were slaves and that God heard their cries. Torah reminded the people of Israel that God would hear the cries of those in need whom they failed to help or whom they oppressed.

Just as God helped Israel, so Israel should help those in need. Fields and vineyards were not to be fully harvested so that the poor could come and take the food they needed. (See Leviticus 19:9-10.) Harvested crops mistakenly left in the field were not to be picked up by the owner, but left for the poor. Isaiah equates helping the poor with proper devotion to God—a spiritual discipline such as fasting (Isaiah 58:6-12).

- What does the phrase "where no one gave him anything" indicate about the people at the place where the younger son was?
- How have you experienced being in a situation where no one would give you anything? Think not just about physical things, but also emotional needs, for example. How did that feel?

Desperate, he takes a job tending swine, about as low as an observant Jew could go. It wasn't a matter of it being dirty work. The son grew up on a farm and presumably had been dirty at times from working in the fields and tending animals. But tending pigs was prohibited for a Jew, and to be forced to care for the swine would have seemed like a curse.

- Do you know someone who is in a place where no one would give him or her anything? or who has been reduced to doing things that are offensive just to survive?
- How can you reach out to that person?
- How can Christians make a change in society so that more people have the basic help they need to survive, without having to resort to activities that are demeaning?

AFTER LOOKING AT BOTH THE TEXT AND THE CONTEXT . . .

> Deal with some or all of these questions before moving to What's Next?

- What new insights do you have?

- What stands out to you in the story now?

- What answers have you gained to the questions you raised earlier?

- What new questions do you have?

- In what ways do you identify with the younger son? with the father? with the older son?

- How do you respond to perceived favoritism within your family?

- How easily are you able to celebrate, without jealousy, the good things that happen to someone else in your family? or among your good friends?

- What one learning do you take from this Scripture that you will remember and apply to your life?

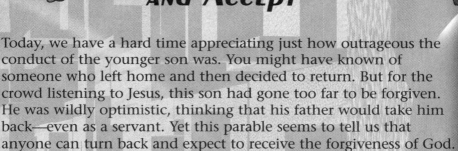

Choose one or more of Views A, B, and C to discuss; **OR** have different small groups talk about one and then summarize the discussion for the other groups. **Be sure to have everyone complete View You.**

VIEW A — REPENT AND ACCEPT

Today, we have a hard time appreciating just how outrageous the conduct of the younger son was. You might have known of someone who left home and then decided to return. But for the crowd listening to Jesus, this son had gone too far to be forgiven. He was wildly optimistic, thinking that his father would take him back—even as a servant. Yet this parable seems to tell us that anyone can turn back and expect to receive the forgiveness of God.

- Who are some people you would consider to have committed acts that are unforgivable?
- Historical figures such as Adolph Hitler, confessed murderers, child molesters, and so forth might come to mind. On its face, this parable tells us that any one of these persons can repent and return to God, expecting to be forgiven by God. How do you feel about that?
- Would you be willing to welcome such persons into your church on the basis of their profession that they have repented and been forgiven by God?
- Does it matter that you can't see into their heart, as long as God can?

Roleplay a conversation between the two brothers (or two sisters or a brother and sister) after the younger's return.

- If you are the younger sibling, what do you say to the older?
- If you are the older, what could the younger sibling say or do to help you come to terms with the situation?
- Are there persons who have cut themselves off from your group? or from your family?
- What have you done to make sure they know that they are welcome to return?

RADICAL JESUS

No One Gave Him Anything

The younger son finds himself in a far land "where no one gave him anything." Think for a moment what it would be like to be somewhere where no one would give you anything.

- Working first in small groups, then as a whole group, list those things that you have been given during your life. Be as expansive in your listing as you can, even considering those things you were given as an infant.
- Now think about what you still might be given before you are on your own as an adult and what you might even receive in the way of gifts after you are an adult.
- Finally, make a list of all persons who have given you gifts.

Douglas Meeks, a theologian, writes that Christianity is a religion based upon "gifting." We profess that, in Jesus Christ, God has given a gift of grace. It is a gift because it is undeserved and unearned. However, Professor Meeks has noted that, as a society, we have all but stopped making gifts to any but members of our families. Today many children are growing up in situations "where no one will give them anything." Their parents have little or nothing to give and fewer and fewer programs are able to make those gifts that these young people need.

- How do you share the gospel of Jesus Christ with someone who has little or no experience with giving or receiving gifts?
- How do you communicate the idea of a gift of grace to someone who has no experience of receiving gifts of any kind?

JUST WHO IS ALLOWED IN, GOD?

Did the younger son truly repent? *Repent* means, literally, to turn. As used in Scripture the word means to turn one's life back toward God. This story is often presented as one in which the younger son repents and turns his life back toward the father character, who represents God.

Professor of religious studies David Buttrick has suggested that there was no repentance in this story. Look again at the conversation the younger son has with himself. He is alone and hungry and recalls that even his father's servants have food. He says "Self, this is what I will do. I will go home and tell Father that I am sorry and ask to be taken back as a lowly servant." Might this plan be what another generation would call a "Soup Line Repentance" (repentance made for the purpose of getting a meal or getting a roof over his head)? Remember, this is the guy who had the gall to demand the inheritance from his father. Such a person might be willing to say anything to be accepted back, especially if he were hungry and alone. Still, the father takes him back, not seemingly even interested in his repentance.

• Do you think the younger brother is truly repentant?
• If not, does that change the meaning of the story?

We profess to believe that all of humanity belongs to God; that all of humanity are children of God, whether they accept Jesus Christ or not. Assume that the elder son represents Christians—those who claim Jesus Christ in their life, however half-heartedly—and the younger son represents those who turn their lives toward God, however half-heartedly, but do not accept Jesus Christ.

• Do we ever act like the elder son when we think of people of other faith traditions, believing that God will not, or should not, accept them into God's kingdom unless they also profess Jesus Christ?
• How would you treat persons differently if you looked at them from the perspective of the father—not of the elder son?

VIEW YOU

As Christians, we acknowledge that we are sinners, even when we repent. We are forgiven sinners, but we still struggle with sin in our lives. Nevertheless, like the father in the story, God has accepted us and continues to work with us on the state of our soul. Spend some time in prayer this week, thinking about the ways you have acted to cut yourself off from God. Pray for God to help you with those things in your life that pull you away from God.

In this space, or on a sheet of paper, write your reflections about this question: How is God speaking to me today through this Word?

The Woman at the Well
John 4:4-42

Whom do you know who is an outsider? Maybe you feel like an outsider—someone to whom others rarely talk. When someone does speak to the outsider, the person who is used to being left out might feel a little uncomfortable or suspicious. Something very like that is going on when Jesus, a male Jewish teacher, encounters a Samaritan woman at a well.

4 [Jesus] had to go through Samaria. 5 So he came to a Samaritan city called Sychar, near the plot of ground that Jacob had given his son Joseph. 6 Jacob's well was there, and Jesus, tired out by his journey, was sitting by the well. It was about noon.

7 A Samaritan woman came to draw water, and Jesus said to her, "Give me a drink." 8 (His disciples had gone to the city to buy food.) 9 The Samaritan woman said to him, "How is it that you, a Jew, ask a drink of me, a woman of Samaria?" (Jews do not share things in common with Samaritans.) 10 Jesus answered her, "If you knew the gift of God, and who it is that is saying to you, 'Give me a drink,' you would have asked him, and he would have given you living water." 11 The woman said to him, "Sir, you have no bucket, and the well is deep. Where do you get that living water? 12 Are you greater than our ancestor Jacob, who gave us the well, and with his sons and his flocks drank from it?" 13 Jesus said to her, "Everyone who drinks of this water will be thirsty again, 14 but those who drink of the water that I will give them will never be thirsty. The water that I will give will become in them a spring of water gushing up to eternal life." 15 The woman said to him, "Sir, give me this water, so that I may never be thirsty or have to keep coming here to draw water."

16 Jesus said to her, "Go, call your husband, and come back." 17 The woman answered him, "I have no husband." Jesus said to her, "You are right in saying, 'I have no husband'; 18 for you have had five husbands, and the one you have now is not your husband. What you have said is true!" 19 The woman said to him, "Sir, I see that you are a prophet. 20 Our ancestors worshiped on this mountain, but you say that the place where people must worship is in Jerusalem." 21 Jesus said to her, "Woman, believe me, the hour is coming when you will worship the Father neither on this mountain nor in Jerusalem. 22 You

worship what you do not know; we worship what we know, for salvation is from the Jews. 23 But the hour is coming, and is now here, when the true worshipers will worship the Father in spirit and truth, for the Father seeks such as these to worship him. 24 God is spirit, and those who worship must worship in spirit and truth." 25 The woman said to him, "I know that Messiah is coming" (who is called Christ). "When he comes, he will proclaim all things to us." 26 Jesus said to her, "I am he, the one who is speaking to you."

27 Just then his disciples came. They were astonished that he was speaking with a woman, but no one said, "What do you want?" or "Why are you speaking with her?" 28 Then the woman left her water jar and went back to the city. She said to the people, 29 "Come and see a man who told me everything I have ever done! He cannot be the Messiah, can he?" 30 They left the city and were on their way to him.

31 Meanwhile the disciples were urging him, "Rabbi, eat something." 32 But he said to them, "I have food to eat that you do not know about." 33 So the disciples said to one another, "Surely no one has brought him something to eat?" 34 Jesus said to them, "My food is to do the will of him who sent me and to complete his work. 35 Do you not say, 'Four months more, then comes the harvest'? But I tell you, look around you, and see how the fields are ripe for harvesting. 36 The reaper is already receiving wages and is gathering fruit for eternal life, so that sower and reaper may rejoice together. 37 For here the saying holds true, 'One sows and another reaps.' 38 I sent you to reap for which you did not labor. Others have labored, and you have entered into their labor."

39 Many Samaritans from that city believed in him because of the woman's testimony, "He told me everything I have ever done." 40 So when the Samaritans came to him, they asked him to stay with them; and he stayed there two days. 41 And many more believed because of his word. 42 They said to the woman, "It is no longer because of what you said that we believe, for we have heard for ourselves, and we know that this is truly the Savior of the world."

John 4:4-42, NRSV

Read the passage aloud. Have everyone highlight words or phrases in the text that they feel are important or that raise questions for them. For now, just list the highlighted words and phrases and the questions.

In small groups or pairs make a list of the actions and issues in sequence for these passages: 4-15, 16-26, 27-38, 39-42. Use a marker and a large sheet of paper.

In the same small groups, use a different color marker and write near the action or issue the emotions of the people involved.

Come together and review the actions, issues, and emotions of the whole story.

- If there were different ideas as to the issues or emotions, what new understandings do you gain from the different perspectives?
- What stood out in the story that you didn't think about earlier?
- What new questions does this experience with the text raise for you?

Add the new highlights and questions to the list.

WHAT'S THE CONTEXT?

As a whole group, read through this information and discuss the questions; **OR** read and discuss the commentaries in small groups or pairs assigned to a specific section or sections. Then summarize your conversation for the others.

The Gospel of John

The Gospels of Matthew, Mark, and Luke are sometimes referred to as the *synoptic* gospels. *Synoptic* means "seen together." Matthew, Mark, and Luke all contain similar material about Jesus, including some accounts that are nearly identical. Most scholars believe that Matthew and Luke both relied heavily upon the Gospel of Mark as a source. The Gospel of John, however, is quite different.

• Use a Bible that has headings and gives cross references to similar texts. Do a quick comparison of any one of the synoptic Gospels with John. Look for these things. Where do they occur—or not?

  Kingdom of God parables, birth narratives, temptation of Christ, Jesus praying in the garden to avoid crucifixion

John's portrayal of Jesus is also somewhat different. More than in any other Gospel, Jesus is shown as being all-knowing—someone who knows what others are thinking and who seems to know what will happen next. Also, Jesus often identifies himself as the Son of God and speaks in terms of others needing to believe in him.

• Read John 1:1-14. Who is "the Word of God made flesh"?
• Read Genesis 1:1-5. What similarities do you notice with the John passage?
• What claim is John making about the Word in relationship to the power of God, which brought everything into being in Creation?
• What is John's primary focus in writing this Gospel? See John 20:31.

RADICAL JESUS

JEWS AND SAMARITANS

- Recall Jesus' parable of the good Samaritan (Luke 10:25-37). Why was that such a radical story for him to have told?
- How did Jews and Samaritans feel about one another? Why?

After the death of King Solomon, Israel was split into two kingdoms. The Northern Kingdom continued to be called Israel. Its capital was Samaria. In the South was the kingdom of Judah, with its capital at Jerusalem. Politically, the two kingdoms were separate. Religiously, they were "family"—one people.

However, the Temple built by Solomon was located in Jerusalem. In order to keep his people from worshiping at the Temple in Jerusalem, and possibly being influenced by the kingdom of Judah, King Jeroboam of Israel built a shrine at Shechem. At this time, the religious practices of Jews in Israel were not significantly different from those in Judah, except for the crucial difference that those in Israel did not worship at the Jerusalem Temple. In Scripture, this practice is immediately condemned by a prophet from Judah (1 Kings 13:1-10).

When the Assyrians invaded and destroyed the city of Samaria in 722 B.C., effectively destroying the Northern Kingdom, they took many of the inhabitants into captivity, replacing them with people from other lands. The remaining people of Samaria, many of whom were foreigners, began worshiping in ways that were incompatible with the understanding of the Jews of Judah. Most notably, at some point, they built a place of worship on Mt. Gerizim. Even after that temple was destroyed, it remained a point of contention between these two people.

By Jesus' day, there was open hatred between the two groups. The hatred between Jews and Samaritans was so intense that male Jews had a prayer thanking God that they had not been born a woman or a Samaritan.

- Religious disputes between people with otherwise similar backgrounds are fairly common, even today. What disputes do you know about between groups of people that are based, at least in part, on religious differences? Why do you think they happen?

Men and Women at a Well

Any group of Jews hearing a story that begins with Jesus encountering a woman at a well would likely remember the role that such encounters played in the history of the covenant people.

- Read the following passages:

  Genesis 24:10-61 (Isaac's servant was sent to find a wife for Isaac.)
  Genesis 29:1-10 (Jacob meets Rachel.)
  Exodus 2:15b-21 (Moses meets Zipporah.)

Marriage imagery is used a number of times in the Old Testament to describe the covenant relationship between Israel and God. (See, for example, Isaiah 54:5; Jeremiah 2:2; Hosea 2:16.) John the Baptist uses such imagery when speaking of Jesus as the bridegroom and John the Baptist as the bridegroom's friend (John 3:29).

- How might the marriage imagery suggested by an encounter at the well relate to the events described in this Scripture passage?

WOMEN IN MINISTRY

Another controversial aspect of this encounter is the fact that Jesus is conversing with the woman at all. Such openness between men and women is so radical that John records the woman's comment about it and makes a point of telling us that it was a breach of custom. Jesus is a Jewish teacher and a man; the woman is a Samaritan. Male Jews would not, as a rule, in that place and time, speak to a woman who was not known to them; and a Jewish teacher would not speak to a woman at all—especially a Samaritan.

• Why do you think Jesus was willing to go against custom?

The passage dealing with the woman's past has occasioned much speculation about her behavior. Some believe that she may have been a prostitute or otherwise morally questionable. However, it is important to note that Jesus makes no such moral judgments about her, and some commentators have pointed out the woman could have been married several times and be living with a man not her husband, without violating any customs of that culture or living an immoral life. The important thing that John would have us understand is that there are no secrets from Jesus. Jesus knows all there is to know about us, whether good or bad.

• Do you agree or disagree that Jesus knows all there is about you? Why?

The unnamed Samaritan woman is one of the first persons to proclaim Jesus as the Messiah. That makes her one of the first evangelists. However, even today in society and in some churches, women are treated with less respect than men, even when they serve as pastors. Some persons feel that women should not be leaders in the church.

• Why do you think those feelings exist?
• How do you think Jesus would respond to criticism of women pastors and church leaders if he appeared today?
• If you are female, have you considered a leadership role in the church now or in the future? How has that idea been received?

Living Water

- Call to mind what you know about the land of the Middle East. Describe it. How important is water in that area?
- How important is water to you? Why?

In Scripture, water is a symbol for the life-giving power of God—as well as the power of God to destroy. God's spirit moves over the waters at Creation, bringing order out of chaos. Water is used to destroy the earth in Noah's story but is used also to sustain the Ark. The people of Israel are delivered through the waters of the Red Sea, but those same waters destroy Pharaoh's army. The psalmist speaks of our souls thirsting for God (Psalm 63:1). Water is the source of our life, just as God is the source of our life.

When Jesus asks the woman for water, she is startled that he should speak to her at all. When he tells her that he can provide "living water," she is both disbelieving and hopeful. The Greek term that is translated as "living water" here can have the meaning of "spring water," and the woman would know that there was no spring nearby. She then seems to think that Jesus is some sort of magician, who can provide water that will permanently quench her thirst. Any inhabitant of an arid land would be interested in such an offer.

- What in this background information surprised you? What was a new understanding for you?
- To get a feel for the give and take of this conversation, have two members of the group roleplay it. Have them read through verses 7-15 once so that they are familiar with it, and then have them read it again as if they were the woman and Jesus.
- What feelings came through in the roleplay?
- What new insight or questions did hearing the exchange give you?

After Looking at Both the Text and the Context . . .

> Deal with some or all of these questions before moving to What's Next?

- What new insights do you have?

- What stands out to you in the story now?

- What answers have you gained to the questions you raised earlier?

- What new questions do you have?

- In what ways do you identify with the woman? with the disciples? with the people in the town?

- Who introduced you to the "living water" of Christ?

- What one learning do you take from this Scripture that you will remember and apply to your life?

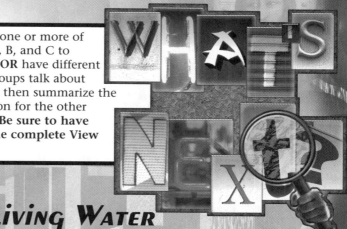

Choose one or more of Views A, B, and C to discuss; **OR** have different small groups talk about one and then summarize the discussion for the other groups. **Be sure to have everyone complete View You.**

VIEW A LIVING WATER

Water is a sustainer of life, a home for life, possibly the place where life first appeared on this planet.

- Make a list of ways water is described in Scripture, symbolically or as an element of a story. (For example, Genesis 1:1-2 describes the waters of the "void" just before the moment of Creation; Naaman, in 2 Kings 5:14, washes in the water and is cleansed of leprosy.)
- One interpretation of the term translated as "living water" would be "flowing water," as from a spring. As you visualize water flowing from a spring, what meaning do you think the writer of the Gospel of John wanted his community to hear in Jesus' words?
- What does this passage about Jesus being "living water" mean to you?
- In what way(s) is Jesus "living water" in the lives of Christians today?
- How well do you trust Jesus to supply you with "living water"?

The Outsiders

The Samaritan woman may be one of the most famous women in literature, but we never learn her name. For the most part, women were not persons of authority or importance in the First Century Middle East. Jesus was breaking with the norm in speaking with a woman. But because Jesus took the time to converse with her, the Gospel spread. Indeed, this unnamed woman became one of the very first evangelists.

The woman was also a Samaritan—a group usually shunned by Jews. Samaritans would have felt much the same about Jews. Yet because these two persons put aside their differences to talk to each other, a new understanding took place. A bond was formed—a bond that wouldn't have been formed if Jesus and the woman had honored the status quo and not been so radical.

- Who are the outsiders in your school or community? Who are those people whom you might not hate but with whom you have little contact? Persons of other religions? People of different races? People whose social class is not the same as yours? Identify as many such groups as you can.
- What is it that separates this group of people from you? Geography? Language? Customs? Religion? Economic status? Values?
- What things do you have in common with these different groups? Do you go to the same school? Do you ever attend the same events? Are any of them members of your church? or of another?
- How difficult would it be for you to get to know some of the people in these different groups?
- How might you do that? Work out a plan to get to know some of these people with whom you have had little contact.

The Fractured Body of Christ

The woman says to Jesus, "Our ancestors [the Samaritans] worshiped on this mountain, but you [Jews] say that the place where people must worship is in Jerusalem." It seems like a small difference, doesn't it? Yet the Christian church is fractured by the same sort of controversies today.

Working as a group, list all of the different Christian traditions you are aware of in your area. (A phone book might help you out.) Ask who of your group knows people in these traditions. Try to identify areas where you think there is disagreement in teachings or beliefs. (For example, someone from another tradition may hold beliefs about baptism that are different from yours.) Your pastor may be able to help with this. Use these questions to help focus the discussion:

- What do the different traditions believe about baptism? about the purpose and effect of the sacrament of Communion?
- How many sacraments are celebrated in the various traditions?
- What are the teachings and beliefs about the authority and inerrancy of Scripture?
- What beliefs and practices do most of the traditions hold in common?
- John Wesley, the founder of Methodism, once said that no one holds a belief, thinking that it is wrong; but that does not make his or her belief correct. What do you think Jesus might have said about all of the differences in belief among the Christian traditions?
- What kinds of experiences have you had in discussing Christian belief and practice with persons of other traditions? How well have you and they been able to set aside differences in understandings and be followers of Jesus together? Why?

View You

We cannot live without water. If we try, we die. This passage tells us that God is like the water we need to live. Without God in our lives, without God's living water, we die. Spend some time in prayer about your thirst for the living water of God.

You might find it helpful to meditate on a glass or bowl of water to help you focus. Reflect on and pray about those times in your life when you have tried to live without the life-giving water of God's grace. See yourself drinking deeply from the water.

Turn your prayers to those people you see as outsiders. Ask Christ to help you see these people as God sees them. See yourself sharing the water with them.

In this space, or on a sheet of paper, write your reflections about this question: How is God speaking to me today through this Word?

Doubting Thomas
John 20:19-29

Have you ever been so frightened, so afraid, that you shut yourself away in a room and locked the door? If so, don't feel alone. Many people have been that frightened at different times in their lives. At such times, it can be hard to believe in God, in Jesus— hard to believe that Jesus is with you, close to you. But, Scripture tells us that Jesus not only finds us in those locked rooms, but he comes in with a list of things we need to do . . . outside.

19 When it was evening on that day, the first day of the week, and the doors of the house where the disciples had met were locked for fear of the Jews, Jesus came and stood among them and said, "Peace be with you." 20 After he said this, he showed them his hands and his side. Then the disciples rejoiced when they saw the Lord. 21 Jesus said to them again, "Peace be with you. As the Father has sent me, so I send you." 22 When he had said this, he breathed on them and said to them, "Receive the Holy Spirit. 23 If you forgive the sins of any, they are forgiven them; if you retain the sins of any, they are retained."

24 But Thomas (who was called the Twin), one of the twelve, was not with them when Jesus came. 25 So the other disciples told him, "We have seen the Lord." But he said to them, "Unless I see the mark of the nails in his hands, and put my finger in the mark of the nails and my hand in his side, I will not believe."

26 A week later his disciples were again in the house, and Thomas was with them. Although the doors were shut, Jesus came and stood among them and said, "Peace be with you." 27 Then he said to Thomas, "Put your finger here and see my hands. Reach out your hand and put it in my side. Do not doubt but believe." 28 Thomas answered him, "My Lord and my God!" 29 Jesus said to him, "Have you believed because you have seen me? Blessed are those who have not seen and yet have come to believe."

John 20:19-29, NRSV

Read the passage aloud. Have others read the passage in different translations.

- What differences are there?
- How do the differences help you understand the text?
- What questions do the differences raise for you?

Have everyone highlight words or phrases in the text that they feel are important or that raise questions for them. For now, just list the highlighted words and phrases and the questions.

Do three quick roleplays: verses 19-23, 24-25, and 26-29. Or draw pictures of some aspect of the story and present it to the group.

- What stood out in the story that you didn't think about earlier?
- What new questions does this experience with the text raise for you?

Add the new highlights and questions to the list.

WHAT'S THE CONTEXT?

Before and After

Scan Chapter 20 of the Gospel of John.

- What happened immediately before this passage?
- What do you think was the reaction of the disciples to Mary's story? Read Luke 24:10-11 also. Why might they have had that reaction?
- How do people generally react to something so amazing?

Read verses 30-31, which follow today's story.

- According to John, what are the purposes of the signs and of the book?
- Read John 3:16. How does this passage relate to the purposes?
- How might "life" (verse 31) and "eternal life" (verse 16) be the same? How might they be different?

- After reading all of Chapter 20, about what would you say John is passionate? What does he want his readers to do and experience?

RESURRECTION APPEARANCES of JESUS

One of the earliest scriptural references to the Resurrection of Jesus is found in 1 Corinthians 15:3-8. There, the apostle Paul, writing at a time well before any of the Gospels were written, recounts what he has been taught by the church:

For I handed on to you as of first importance what I in turn had received: that Christ died for our sins in accordance with the scriptures, and that he was buried, and that he was raised on the third day in accordance with the scriptures, and that he appeared to Cephas [Peter], then to the twelve. Then he appeared to more than five hundred brothers and sisters at one time, most of whom are still alive, though some have died. Then he appeared to James, then to all the apostles. Last of all, as to one untimely born, he appeared also to me. [Paul is referring to his encounter with Jesus on the road to Damascus (Acts 9:1-8).]

• What surprises you about this information from Paul? What is new information for you?

Scan the story in John 21:1-14 (and the Resurrection appearances, if you have time, in Matthew 28:1-10; 16-20; and Luke 24:13-35).

• How would you have felt if you had been present then?

The Resurrection of Christ from the dead is a central belief of Christianity. We proclaim that

- • In Jesus Christ, God became flesh and blood—the Word made flesh.
- • We (sinful humanity) did our best to kill the Word of God in our midst. Christ, in turn, sacrificed himself for the forgiveness of our sin.
- • God, through the Resurrection demonstrated that God's grace is more powerful than our ability to sin.
- • God is with us wherever we are, in life, in death, in life beyond death.

• Which of these beliefs do you have some doubts about?
• Is doubting or questioning wrong? Why, or why not?

RADICAL JESUS

Afraid of the Jews?

Were the disciples afraid of the Jews? That assertion is problematic. Jesus was crucified by the Romans. Crucifixion was a Roman form of punishment, and the Romans were more than willing to use terror to control a population. Pilate's brutal nature is documented outside the Bible. There would have been good reason for the disciples to fear being picked up by Roman authorities. There would have been less reason to fear the Jews.

For the most part, the earliest disciples were Jews. However, as the Christian movement grew, so did conflicts between Christian Jews and other Jews. Many commentators believe that it is those tensions that caused the writer of John to portray the disciples here as fearing "the Jews."

A sad part of our history has been the persecution of Jews by Christians. Some references in Scripture, like the one above, feed the fears of some people and can lead some Christians to dislike or even hate Jews.

- Assume that the early disciples did fear persecution by some of the Jewish leaders in Jerusalem. How should that information affect the way modern Christians interact with Jews and people of other religious traditions?
- What do you know from history about anti-Semitism (prejudice against Jews) and its results?
- What are relationships between Christians and Jews like in your community? in your school? Why?
- How might they be improved, if need be?

If you have time, read Romans 11:17-24.

- How does this passage relate to the question of how Christians should relate to Jews?

The Holy Spirit

Most people are familiar with the story of the giving of the Holy Spirit on Pentecost, described in Acts. Many people are surprised by this description in the Gospel of John. Read Acts 2:1-4. Compare the two accounts of the giving of the Holy Spirit to the church.

• What is the same? What is different?
• Which account do you find more meaningful? Why?

When Jesus "breathes" on the disciples, they receive the Holy Spirit. Interestingly, the Hebrew and Greek words translated as "Spirit" also have the meaning of "wind" or "breath." Jesus' act of breathing on the disciples was a commissioning of them to be the church, to carry on Jesus' work in the world (verse 23).

• Did God's Holy Spirit come into action only in this or the Acts story? Check out Genesis 1:30 and 2:7; Psalm 33:6; Jeremiah 10:14.
• What is the significance of the word *breath* in each of these passages? How is it used?
• Why is forgiving what the church is commissioned to do? Why would it be central to the church's ministry in the world?

Resurrection and the Kingdom

Resurrection from the dead is a sign in Jewish apocalyptic literature that the "End Times" have arrived and that a new era of God's Reign, God's Kingdom, has begun on earth (Isaiah 26:19 and Daniel 12:2). The Gospel of Matthew even describes others, Jewish saints, whom he claims were raised from the dead by the power of Jesus' sacrifice on the cross (Matthew 27:51-53). Paul describes Christ as the first to be resurrected of those who have died (1 Corinthians 15:20-23).

A popular series of books talks about the "End Times" as if they have not yet arrived. But others would contend that the "End Times" began with the resurrection of Christ, that, indeed, the kingdom of God has begun.

• What do you think?

AFTER LOOKING AT BOTH THE TEXT AND THE CONTEXT . . .

> Deal with some or all of these questions before moving to What's Next?

- What new insights do you have?

- What stands out to you in the story now?

- What answers have you gained to the questions you raised earlier?

- What new questions do you have?

- In what ways do you identify with Thomas?

- How does Jesus treat Thomas?

- How difficult is it for you to believe in a God you can't see?

- How have you experienced the commissioning of Jesus in your life? in your church?

- How has the Holy Spirit been part of the ministry you do? of the ministry of your church?

- What one learning do you take from this Scripture that you will remember and apply to your life?

Choose one or more of Views A, B, and C to discuss; **OR** have different small groups talk about one and then summarize the discussion for the other groups. **Be sure to have everyone complete View You.**

VIEW A — *If Seeing Is Believing, How Do We See Christ?*

The problem of disbelief is not confined to Thomas. Matthew notes that some of the disciples did not believe that Christ was raised from the dead (Matthew 28:17), and Paul is apparently addressing such questions in 1 Corinthians 15. Other people also had explanations for the disappearance of the body (Matthew 28:11-15). Finally, in this age of reason and logic, many people inside and outside the church question the accounts of the Resurrection appearances.

- Take a few minutes to talk about the Resurrection; explore people's feelings and beliefs about it. As you do so, remember that doubt is always part of faith. If we have ironclad proof about something, it is no longer a matter of faith. And as we see with Thomas, Jesus does not condemn those who have doubts.

Have someone read aloud Psalm 139:1-18 and Matthew 28:20b.

- What assurance do these Scriptures give you?
- Have you or anyone else in the group had an experience of the living presence of Christ in their life? What was it like?

In addition to the inward assurance, the apostle Paul reminds us that the church, through the power of God's Spirit, is the body of Christ—the living presence of Christ on earth.

- How have you seen the risen Christ in the work and presence of the church?

RADICAL JESUS

87

 B ## Locked Rooms and Jesus

Christianity is a religion that calls upon us to be in the world. But sometimes, like the disciples, we tend to shut ourselves away from the world, both individually and as whole congregations.

- What things make you want to retreat from the world?
- What types of experiences have you had that have made you want to shut yourself away in a room for a while?
- In what ways can a whole congregation, in effect, shut itself away from the world? What sorts of factors lead to such situations?

Presumably, the disciples were afraid to let others know that they were followers of Jesus.

- Is that a problem for you today? Do you fear letting people know that you are Christian?

A powerful image in this text is Jesus' walking into the closed room and breathing the Spirit of God onto the disciples.

- How does Jesus break into our lives today, calling us back into ministry in the world?
- How have you experienced being called to minister to someone or in some situation?
- Jesus tells the disciples that he is sending them into the world. In what ways does your church send you into the world?

Both of the times Jesus enters the room, he tells the disciples, "Peace be with you."

- How do you experience peace as a follower of Jesus?

THAT RADICAL JESUS

Jesus is both human and divine. He lived and died, but he also rose from the dead and appeared again to those who loved and followed him.

Jesus does not give Thomas grief for wanting proof of the Resurrection. Instead, he gives him what he needs in order to believe—and ultimately to have abundant and eternal life. Encountering Jesus changes lives for the better!

Before Jesus leaves, he commissions not just eleven men, known as the disciples, but the whole community of faith for continuing his work as the church, the body of Christ. And he gives his peace.

Jesus' ministry from the beginning turned the world upside down—and it's not done yet!

- What do you find to be radical about Jesus?
- How do you think he has changed the world? How would life as we know it be different if Jesus had not lived and died and been resurrected?
- What is it like to believe in Jesus—even though we don't see him?
- How easy is it to trust Jesus? Why?

RADICAL JESUS

 **VIEW YOU**

In the Orthodox tradition, the traditional Easter greeting is "Christ is risen!" followed by the response, "He is risen indeed!" Spend some time in meditative prayer, using that phrase as a prayer focus. Repeat it over and over in your mind, like a chant. After a while, move into a time of seeking the spiritual assurance of the truth of these words. The assurance that Christ is indeed risen and with you.

During this prayer time, pray about those things that make you want to retreat from the world. Pray for Christ's help if you have locked yourself away from others.

In this space, or on a sheet of paper, write your reflections about this question: How is God speaking to me today through this Word?